Read & Respond

FOR
KS2

Read & Respond

FOR
KS2

Author: Rob Walton

Editor: Roanne Charles

Assistant Editor: Niamh O'Carroll

Series Designer: Anna Oliwa

Designer: Allison Parry

Cover Image: Chris Riddell

Illustrations: Chantal Kees

Text © 2006 Rob Walton
© 2006 Scholastic Ltd

Designed using Adobe InDesign

Published by Scholastic Ltd, Villiers House,
Clarendon Avenue, Leamington Spa,
Warwickshire CV32 5PR

www.scholastic.co.uk

Printed by Bell & Bain

1 2 3 4 5 6 7 8 9   6 7 8 9 0 1 2 3 4 5

British Library Cataloguing-in-Publication Data
A catalogue record for this book is available from the British
Library.

ISBN 0-439-96580-2   ISBN 978-0439-96580-4

Acknowledgements
Chantal Kees for the use of illustrations from *Read and
Respond: The Sheep-Pig* © 1997, Chantal Kees (1997, Scholastic
Limited). **The Penguin Group (UK)** for the use of extracts from
The Sheep-Pig by Dick King-Smith © 1983 Fox Busters Ltd
(1983, Victor Gollancz).

The Sheep-Pig

About the book

The Sheep-Pig has been a hugely successful book because it is an imaginative, funny and heart-warming story. It tells the tale of a very polite piglet who grows up wanting to be a sheep-dog. With the help of one of the farm's existing sheep-dogs, the sheep and the farmer, the pig's dream moves nearer to becoming reality.

Dick King-Smith creates hugely engaging characters and there are many humorous parts to the story, and also sections that are extremely moving. The language and descriptions in the novel are very rich, and there is a great deal of exciting action that makes the reader want to read on. The story takes us into the world of farming, which may be unfamiliar to less rural readers, and to the wonderfully imaginative world of a top children's writer at the peak of his powers.

The Sheep-Pig relates to several NLS genres which include: Year 3 Term 1, stories with familiar settings; Year 3 Term 2, stories with related themes; Year 4 Term 3, stories that raise issues; and Year 5 Term 1, stories by significant children's writers.

In 1995, the book was made into the hugely successful Oscar-winning film *Babe* and a play in 1997.

Plot summary

Farmer Hogget wins a baby pig in a guess-the-weight competition at the village fair. His wife thinks they will fatten the pig up and eat him at Christmas. The pig, named Babe, is fostered by a working sheep-dog, Fly, and befriended by an old sheep, Ma. Babe watches Fly as she herds the sheep, and decides he wants to do it for himself. He is very polite to the sheep and they respond well to this. They also respect him because he chases away a gang of sheep thieves. Gradually, he becomes better at being a sheep-pig and Farmer Hogget enters him for the national Sheep-Dog Trials, where he is the final competitor…

About the author

Dick King-Smith was born in 1922 in Gloucestershire and since then he has been surrounded by animals. He worked as a farmer for 20 years, before becoming a primary school teacher, and then a writer of books for children. He has also, at different times, been a soldier, a salesman and a factory worker. He has written over 30 books for children and enjoys meeting the children who have read them. His first published book, *The Fox Busters*, was written in his 50s, and since then he has continued to write many stories about animals. *The Sheep-Pig* is his most well-known book, and also his own favourite. He still lives just a few miles from where he was born, and says that he does his hobby for a living.

Facts and figures
The Sheep-Pig was first published in 1983. Since then, it has gone on to sell 1,300,000 copies in English language editions and been translated into 12 languages.
The Sheep-Pig was the winner of the 1984 Guardian Fiction Award.

Dick King-Smith photograph © Fred Pryor, Michael Dyer Associates

Guided reading

Chapter 1

Read the first pages until the break at '"Yes," said Farmer Hogget.' Ask the children if they can predict why the chapter title is 'Guess my weight'. Who do they think is being referred to here?

Continue reading from 'When he had driven…' Ask the class what they notice about this sentence. (It is a whole paragraph itself, has long, subordinate clauses, lots of detail, and describes the setting using sounds as well as sights.)

What are the children's first impressions of Farmer and Mrs Hogget? Do they find them likeable, sympathetic, funny? What differences do they notice in the way they speak? (Mrs Hogget is very talkative, Mr Hogget much more reserved and taciturn.)

At the end of the chapter, ask the children who might be on the other end of the telephone and what he or she might be saying. Why do they think the author has placed this phone conversation at this point in the story? (It is directly after Mrs Hogget's comments about eating the parts of a pig, it implies a secret that the reader is let in on.)

Chapters 2 and 3

Begin Chapter 2 and ask the class to identify which new characters are introduced. (Fly and the puppies.) Read the first few pages, until '…crying "Wolf! Wolf!" in their empty-headed way.' Encourage the children to note the variety of exclamation and question marks over the next couple of pages. What does this suggest to them about the story? (It is lively and funny, the questions will elicit information for the reader.) Ask the children which sentence about Fly shows a turning point in the plot. ('At that instant the collie bitch made up her mind that she would foster this unhappy child.') Point out the brevity of Farmer Hogget's exclamations and commands on the last page: 'Pity. Really'; 'Fly!'; 'Sit!'

What is significant about the final line of Chapter 3, 'Why can't I learn to be a sheep-pig?' (First use of phrase, sets up what is to follow.)

Chapter 4

Look at the title of Chapter 4 – 'You'm a Polite Young Chap'. Ask the children what they have noticed about the chapter headings. (They are quotes from the characters.) Ask them if they can predict the theme for this chapter based on the heading.

Begin reading the chapter together. Focus on the second sentence. It is another long one, using alliteration: 'sat', 'squattered', 'splattered', 'soupy'. Ask the children if they have heard the word 'squattered' before. (The author invented it.) Discuss its meaning and that it was invented because nothing else was quite suitable.

Read on and ask the children why Babe is referred to as Fly's foster-child. Some commentators have suggested that adoption is an important theme in the book. Ask the children if they agree, and if they can justify their opinions with reference to the text.

This chapter introduces technical language ('Away to me' and 'Come by'). Challenge the children to read the explanation, then cover the text and recall the meanings of these terms. Can they invent some other plausible commands for shepherding animals? Why do they think Babe is said to have a 'see-sawing canter'? (His short legs and big body make a rocking motion.)

Ask the children why there is a space between the paragraphs after Fly's sentence beginning 'Pigs are intelligent too…' (It indicates a passage of time, continuing on the same theme, as opposed to a chapter break where the theme may change.) Encourage the children to flick through the book to see when this next occurs, and see if this occurrence backs up the theory.

Chapter 5

Begin reading Chapter 5. Ask a volunteer to read out Mrs Hogget's first speech. Ask the children what they notice about the punctuation here. What does this tell them about how she speaks? (A shortage of commas indicate that she barely pauses for breath.) Point out the contrast between this speech and the response from Hogget.

Guided reading

Ask the children to read on for themselves. Draw attention to the sentence 'At the top of the hill a cattle-lorry stood…' Can the children predict what is likely to happen next? Can they find a clue in the chapter title?

Read the final page of the chapter, when Hogget returns from market. What do the children think is grammatically incorrect about Mrs Hogget's 'You won't never believe it!'? (It is a double negative.) Challenge them to 'correct' it. Notice the play on words in the line in Mrs Hogget's final speech '…he saved our bacon and now I'm going to save his…' What do the children think is the significance of this line in terms of the story? (Farmer and Mrs Hogget have arrived at the same conclusion: Babe will not be fattened up for the table.)

Chapter 6

Ask the children to begin reading the chapter, thinking about manners and politeness. Ask them if they think Fly is polite. Discuss her attitude to the sheep – that she feels superior and tries to boss them around. Point out another play on words in the phrase 'woolly heads' and elicit its double meaning.

Read the sentence beginning 'Suddenly, quick as a flash…' Ask the children which verb in this sentence suggests speed. ('sprang'.) Help them to appreciate the author's use of the phrases 'ran helter-skelter' and 'pell-mell' to suggest speed, confusion, and a lack of discipline – usual when Fly herds the sheep. Ask the children to explain in their own words what aspect of shepherding suits Farmer Hogget. (He has to use only a few words to give commands.)

Ask the children to read on, noticing how politely Babe speaks to the sheep. Discuss the phrases he uses, such as 'Good morning! I do hope I find you all well…' At the end of the chapter, point out Hogget's thought '…he's better than a dog! I wonder…!' What does this tell the children about what might follow. (Hogget is beginning to think about training Babe to work with the sheep; he is also perhaps thinking about the Grand Challenge Sheep Dog Trials.)

Chapter 8

Ask the children why Fly is suspicious of Hogget's intentions towards Babe. (She thinks he is grooming Babe to become a sheep-pig for the Trials.) Look at the first paragraph, and ask the children what the phrase 'studded with hazards to be negotiated' means. What do they think might stand in the way of Babe's success as a sheep-pig? (His lack of speed.) Can they find two things that are done to improve Babe's fitness? Ask the children why the author writes 'And the day came when that strength and hardness were to stand him in good stead'? (He is setting up a later scene in the chapter, giving the reader a clue about what is to follow.)

Ask the children to read the rest of the chapter.

Chapter 9

Ask the children what they notice about the beginning of this chapter and the end of the previous one. (They are continuous in terms of time and content. Chapters 1–2 and 11–12 are also continuous.) Establish the meaning of the word bewildered and why it applies to Babe. (He is confused – he doesn't understand the change in attitude towards him. He doesn't know what we know; nor does Farmer Hogget.) Ask the children how Farmer Hogget feels at this point of the story. Is he confused, disappointed, disbelieving? How do the children feel as readers at this tension-packed part of the story? Are they worried for Babe, hoping the farmer will realise what has happened? Read the first few pages and discuss how the mood changes. Draw a parallel between the significant phone call in this chapter and the life-changing one in Chapter 1.

Chapter 10

Look at the first four paragraphs and ask the children what they notice about the beginning of each paragraph. Why do they think the author has used this repetition of 'Because'? Discuss that it is a powerful way of getting information across, rhythm in the repetition makes it interesting to read. Repetition also adds emphasis and reminds us that a lot has happened so far.

Read up to 'Never in his working life…' Discuss how in this sentence the author is sowing the seeds of the next stage in the plot. Point out that the next sentence talks about Farmer Hogget's ambition. Ask if this is the first time they have noticed this aspect of his character. (He has previously been seen as very laid-back and comfortable with his 'lot'. But although he is a reserved man, we now see that he has always wanted to compete in the Trials and now finally thinks he has a chance to make his mark.)

Read on to the next ellipsis. Discuss whether it is fair and honest of Hogget to enter those details on the form for the Trials. Can they see his point of view? What would they feel if they were one of his competitors?

Chapter 12

Ask the children what significance they think the chapter title ('That'll Do') might have? (They are the closing words of the book, tying things together simply, and without sentiment, in a manner appropriate to Farmer Hogget's understated praise of Babe.) Discuss whether this could reflect that the author is not sentimental about animals, instead he is matter-of-fact and imaginative.

Read the opening sentence and ask the children to explain how so many pairs of eyes can watch the Trials. (It is being televised.) In the fifth paragraph, specific places in Britain are mentioned – ask if this is for the first time. (Yes). Have the children had their own image of the country setting for the story? There are many possibilities – the film is effortlessly relocated to Australia for example. Sheep farming takes place all over the world and this is part of the worldwide appeal and success of the novel.

Ask the children to look at the description of Babe as he enters the arena. Notice language features such as adjectives: 'long, lean, beautifully clean', 'great ears fanned, little eyes'; similes: 'stood like a statue'; and the adverb in 'waiting patiently'. Ask them if they see how the spectators' attitudes towards Babe change. (The responses change from laughter and derision, to appreciation of his precision, how quickly he moves and so on.) Ask them to find the polite aside Babe makes about the sheep collars, 'how nice they look, by the way'. Finally, ask how the author uses the weather to illustrate 'the magic of the moment'? (With 'a single shaft of sunshine came suddenly through a hole in the grey clouds…').

Shared reading

Extract 1

- Read the extract together and invite suggestions about the themes it introduces, such as friendship and politeness.
- Explore what causes the relationship between Babe and Ma to develop so quickly. (Babe's civility and friendliness.) Ask the children to circle the words that refer to this ('politely', 'nice name', 'civil', 'kind word').
- Ask the children to underline any unfamiliar vocabulary and see if they can work out the meaning from the context; 'maa-ing,' for example, is invented: do the children think it funny/effective? What does 'tipped a drench' mean? How could a throat be said to 'protest'?
- Ask the children why they think Babe doesn't tell Fly about his conversation with Ma. (He suspects that Fly doesn't think very highly of the sheep; she thinks they are stupid, and so wouldn't approve of him befriending one of them.)
- Ask the children to find the short word repeated three times halfway through the extract ('all'). Discuss the effect of this repetition in heightening the effect of the dream. Do the children think the phrase 'hatred gleaming in their mad yellow eyes' suggests a dream or a nightmare? Can they imagine it?

Extract 2

- Ask the children to read the extract with you. Do they recognise which part of the book it comes from? (The beginning.) Do they find the use of a direct question for the opening sentence effective? Why?
- Ask the children to find the apostrophes in Mrs Hogget's first speech, and identify why they are used. (For omission/contraction.)
- Focus on the description of Mrs Hogget's face. The use of 'comfortable' is an unusual choice, but effective in giving us an impression of her.
- Point out the repetition and alliteration in Mrs Hogget's second sentence ('What a racket, what a row') and note the emphatic effect this has.
- Ask the children to circle examples of dialect or speech that is individual to Mrs Hogget. Her style of speech and the way it is presented, with no full stops, helps with her characterisation.
- Challenge the children to estimate how many words Hogget uses in his four sentences (nine in total). Note that this helps with *his* characterisation and contrasts with his wife, making them an interesting couple.
- Point out the short sentence followed by a much longer one in the second paragraph. Discuss the rhythm and interest created and ask the children to consider how they could use this style in their own writing.

Extract 3

- Read the extract together and encourage the children to identify the point in the story. (Hogget intends to kill Babe.) What action has preceded this? (Ma's death, which Hogget thinks Babe was responsible for.)
- Notice how the author changes the mood as events change. At the beginning there is a dark interior and a black gun. Near the end of the extract there is sunlight. Hogget's voice at the beginning is 'cold' and at the end it is 'warm and kindly'. Why has it changed?
- Discuss the black humour in 'some quite unexpected surprise would come out of its two small round mouths'. (Make sure the children understand this refers to Babe's trusting nature and the fact that pigs like to eat.)
- Ask the children to find and explain the evidence Hogget has that Babe has been a hero. (The hairs around Babe's mouth are the same colour as the sheep-worrying dogs.)

Extract 1

"My name's Babe," he said in a jolly voice. "What's yours?"

"Maaaaa," said the sheep.

"That's a nice name," said Babe. "What's the matter with you, Ma?"

"Foot-rot," said the sheep, holding up a foreleg. "And I've got a nasty cough." She coughed. "And I'm not as young as I was."

"You don't look very old to me," said Babe politely.

A look of pleasure came over the sheep's mournful face, and she lay down in the straw.

"Very civil of you to say so," she said. "First kind word I've had since I were a little lamb," and she belched loudly and began to chew a mouthful of cud.

Though he did not quite know why, Babe said nothing to Fly of his conversation with Ma. Farmer Hogget had treated the sheep's foot and tipped a drench down its protesting throat, and now, as darkness fell, dog and pig lay side by side, their rest only occasionally disturbed by a rustling from the next-door box. Having at last set eyes on a sheep, Babe's dreams were immediately filled with the creatures, all lame, all coughing, all, like the ducks, scattering wildly before his attempts to round them up.

"Go here, go there, do this, do that!" he squeaked furiously at them, but they took not a bit of notice, until at last the dream turned to nightmare, and they all came hopping and hacking and maa-ing after him with hatred gleaming in their mad yellow eyes.

"Mum! Mum!" shouted Babe in terror.

"Maaaaa!" said a voice next door.

"It's all right, dear," said Fly, "it's all right. Was it a nasty dream?"

Extract 2

"What's that noise?" said Mrs Hogget, sticking her comfortable round red face out of the kitchen window. "Listen, there 'tis again, did you hear it, what a racket, what a row, anybody'd think someone was being murdered, oh dearie me, whatever is it, just listen to it, will you?"

Farmer Hogget listened. From the usually quiet valley below the farm came a medley of sounds: the oompah oompah of a brass band, the shouts of children, the rattle and thump of a skittle alley, and every now and then a very high, very loud, very angry-sounding squealing lasting perhaps ten seconds.

Farmer Hogget pulled out an old pocket-watch as big round as a saucer and looked at it. "Fair starts at two," he said. "It's started."

"I knows that," said Mrs Hogget, "because I'm late now with all theseyer cakes and jams and pickles and preserves as is meant to be on the Produce Stall this very minute, and who's going to take them there, I'd like to know, why you are, but afore you does, what's that noise?"

The squealing sounded again.

"That noise?"

Mrs Hogget nodded a great many times. Everything that she did was done at great length, whether it was speaking or simply nodding her head. Farmer Hogget, on the other hand, never wasted his energies or his words.

"Pig," he said.

Mrs Hogget nodded a lot more.

Extract 3

"Come, Pig," said Farmer Hogget in that same cold voice, and strode past him into the stables, while at the same moment, inside the farmhouse, the telephone began to ring, and then stopped as Mrs Hogget picked it up.

Obediently Babe followed the farmer into the dark interior. It was not so dark however that he could not see clearly that the boss was pointing the black shiny tube at him, and he sat down again and waited, supposing that perhaps it was some machine for giving out food and that some quite unexpected surprise would come out of its two small round mouths, held now quite close to his face.

At that instant Mrs Hogget's voice sounded across the yard, calling her husband's name from the open kitchen window. He frowned, lowered the shiny tube, and poked his head a round the stable door.

"Oh there you are!" called Mrs Hogget. "What dost think then, that was the police that was, they'm ringing every farmer in the district to warn 'em, there's sheep-worrying dogs about, they killed six sheep t'other side of the valley only last night, they bin seen they have, two of 'em 'tis, a big black un and a little brown un, they say to shoot 'em on sight if you do see 'em, you better get back up the hill and make sure ours is all right, d'you want me to fetch your gun?"

"No," said Farmer Hogget. "It's all right," he said.

He waited till his wife had shut the window and disappeared, and then he walked out into the sunlight with Babe following.

"Sit, Pig," he said, but now his voice was warm and kindly again.

He looked closely at the trusting face turned up to his, and saw, sticking to the side of Babe's mouth, some hairs, some black hairs, and a few brown ones too.

Plot, character and setting

Character certificates

> **Objective:** To use a range of adjectives.
> **What you need:** Photocopiable page 15, writing materials, flipchart.

What to do

● Revise adjectives and give some example phrases from the text, such as: Hogget is a 'tall, long-striding figure', Babe is 'long, lean, beautifully clean'. Explain that adjectives can be used to describe someone's personality as well as their appearance. For example, as well as being 'tall', Farmer Hogget is 'kind'.

● Ask the children to think of adjectives to describe Babe, Farmer Hogget, Mrs Hogget and Ma. Some from the story are: Babe has 'bright, intelligent eyes', Farmer Hogget has a 'long face', Mrs Hogget has a 'comfortable round red face', Ma has a 'hoarse complaining voice'. Collect a list of suitable adjectives for each character on the flipchart.

● Hand out enough copies of the photocopiable page for the children to write certificates for each of these four characters. Explain that these will be like the certificates they might receive themselves for literacy work or excellent handwriting. Ask why Farmer Hogget might deserve a certificate? (For being kind, thoughtful, patient, and so on.)

● Ask the children to fill in the certificates for each character using phrases and sentences, rather than simply a list of adjectives, such as 'Babe is a polite sheep-pig and a good friend to Ma.'

> **Differentiation**
> **For older/more able children:** The children could make a certificate for Dick King-Smith. They should think about his particular contribution to children's literature, based on *The Sheep-Pig* or any of his other stories they may know.
> **For younger/less able children:** Enlarge one or more of the certificates for the children to complete to give them fewer characters to think about and more space for writing.

Plotting the story

> **Objective:** To explore narrative order.
> **What you need:** Flipchart with headings written on: 'Introduction', 'Build-up', 'Climax/Conflict', 'Resolution'; paper, writing materials.

What to do

● Tell the children that they are going to look at narrative order in *The Sheep-Pig*.

● Use a familiar story, such as *Goldilocks and the Three Bears*, to identify and map out the main parts of a story: introduction to characters, build-up with Goldilocks trying things in the house, climax/conflict with the Bears returning, resolution with Goldilocks running away.

● Now apply the same process to *The Sheep-Pig*. Talk through the introduction (we meet the Hoggets, Babe is won and comes to the farm). Next, ask the children to describe the build-up (Babe is gradually trained as a sheep-pig) and identify any climaxes or conflicts (Babe rescues the sheep, but the Hoggets think initially he has killed Ma). Finally, discuss the resolution (the sheep-dog trials).

● Ask the children to write a plan, in note form, for *The Sheep-Pig* under the four headings. If time allows, they may add more detail, such as other important events. Explain that not everyone will have the same plan, as different readers may think of different climaxes.

> **Differentiation**
> **For older/more able children:** Challenge the children to select suitable connectives to link the parts of their plan into a simple narrative.
> **For younger/less able children:** Ask the children to draw a simple storyboard showing the main events of the story.

Plot, character and setting

"Mouthy old thing"

> **Objective:** To understand the basic conventions of standard English.
> **What you need:** Photocopiable page 16, writing materials, flipchart.

What to do

● Discuss standard English with the children, and whether they think any of the characters in *The Sheep-Pig* speak it. (It tends to be the animals, such as Babe and Fly, who speak standard English.) By contrast, Farmer and Mrs Hogget use dialect – a regional variation of a language used in speech.

● Ask the children why it is important to know the difference, and when it is appropriate to use each one. For example, the narrative of the book is written in standard English. Record the group's thoughts on the flipchart.

● Read through the photocopiable sheet together. Discuss Mrs Hogget's use of English. What are the main features the children notice? (As well

as using dialect, she talks *a lot,* and quickly, and uses more words than necessary. It is the pace and verbosity that hint at her characteristics more than her use of dialect. Do the children think the standard English 'translations' will be shorter or longer than Mrs Hogget's?

● Challenge the children to convert Mrs Hogget's speeches into standard English.

● At the end of the exercise, check the words the children have substituted for Mrs Hogget's dialect words. Use their work as a basis for discussion about the positive and negative aspects of using standard English or dialect in various situations. What do we lose from the character by changing it like this?

> **Differentiation**
> **For older/more able children:** Ask the children to extend one of Mrs Hogget's speeches, making it even more verbose.
> **For younger/less able children:** Ask the children to highlight non-standard words and phrases.

Starting a story

> **Objective:** To experiment with alternative ways of opening a story.
> **What you need:** Opening sentence of the book written on flipchart, paper, writing materials.

What to do

● Ask the children if they can remember the very beginning of the book. Elicit that it begins with the words, 'What's that noise?' What is notable about this? (It's a question given in dialogue, which gets the reader involved straight away, and it introduces the central character 'offstage'.)

● Ask the children to suggest other ways of starting a story or chapter. Prompt them with the terms 'action' and 'description' if necessary.

● Model an alternative opening using action. For example, 'The piglet burst out of the box and scampered across the table.' Ask the

children to spend a few minutes working in pairs writing their own opening. Explain that it should be based on 'action', with a dramatic entrance for Babe. Share and discuss some of their ideas.

● Now invite the pairs to choose another way of opening *The Sheep-Pig* (description, action or dialogue) and to write an original opening paragraph.

● Ask some children to read out their openings, and discuss their strengths as a whole group.

> **Differentiation**
> **For older/more able children:** Ask the children to write opening sentences featuring different characters. They should discuss which is the most effective and why.
> **For younger/less able children:** Let the children storyboard different openings, frame by frame, paying attention to detail.

Plot, character and setting

Story themes

> **Objective:** To identify typical story themes.
> **What you need:** Flipchart, copies of *The Sheep-Pig*.

What to do

● Together think of some traditional story themes, such as trials and forfeits, good versus evil, weak versus strong, the wise defeating the foolish.

● In small groups, tell the children to spend two minutes discussing which, if any, of these are present in *The Sheep-Pig*. Ask a member of each group to report back to the class, referring to the text to support their ideas.

● Next, ask the children to suggest other themes present in *The Sheep-Pig*. These may include politeness, communication, friendship, teamwork, self-esteem, determination, family or hard work. Write all the suggestions on the flipchart.

● Ask the groups to rank these in terms of their importance in the story. Share findings to see if there is a consensus. Discuss why certain themes are more important to different people.

● Which characters do the children associate with the different themes? Note these on the flipchart and discuss the results. Does Babe's name appear most often?

> **Differentiation**
> **For older/more able children:** Give the children two minutes to speed-write a list of traditional story themes in *The Sheep-Pig*.
> **For younger/less able children:** Ask the children to draw the main characters and, around each one, write themes associated with them.

Cliffhangers and set-ups

> **Objective:** To understand how chapters in a book are linked together.
> **What you need:** Copies of *The Sheep-Pig*, paper, writing materials.

What to do

● Ask the children how the chapters are connected in *The Sheep-Pig*. Does the author give clues in one chapter, especially near the end, about what might happen in the next?

● Explain that a new chapter often means a change in setting or time. However, in *The Sheep-Pig*, some chapters end with a pivotal event, and the following chapter continues the action. For example, Chapter 8 ends as Farmer Hogget finds Babe next to the dead Ma. Chapter 11 ends as the Trials begin. Ask if the children can remember how Chapters 9 and 12 begin. (Hogget sends Babe back to the farm; the first dog competes in the Trials.)

● Allow two minutes for paired discussion on other ways the chapters close and open, before reporting back to the class.

● See if any of the chapter endings identified are cliffhangers (or 'nailbiters'). Note that as well as cliffhangers, the author sometimes sets up future events at the end of chapters – he gives hints of what is to come.

● Challenge the children to write an alternative ending to Chapter 8. They should retell the events that have happened so far: Babe has been heroic (although it looks different as he has blood on his nose and is standing next to Ma's dead body) and Farmer Hogget arrives. First discuss possible alternatives: perhaps Hogget is angry, but then looks closely at the situation; Hogget goes to extract revenge straight away; Hogget is overcome with sadness.

> **Differentiation**
> **For older/more able children:** Ask the children to write a set-up: introduce something at the end of a chapter that will become significant later.
> **For younger/less able children:** Ask the children to write the closing sentence for a given chapter.

Plot, character and setting

Who's talking?

Objective: To investigate how characters are presented, eg through dialogue.
What you need: Photocopiable page 17, copies of *The Sheep-Pig*, writing materials.

What to do
● Ask the children to think about how dialogue and speech contribute to characterisation in *The Sheep-Pig*. Do they think they would be able to identify the different styles of speech of all the characters in the novel? Which do they think would be easiest to recognise? Mrs Hogget's rambling? Farmer Hogget's short sentences? Babe's politeness?
● Hand out the photocopiable sheet and explain that each bubble contains speech by one of the characters pictured. Suggest that they can work it out by a combination of memory and identifying the idiosyncrasies of the characters' speech. They can also use elimination and common sense. If they are unsure, encourage them to make an educated guess.
● Discuss the responses and the correct answers, as shown here: Mrs Hogget: H and J; Babe: A and E; Fly: B, D and F; Farmer Hogget: C and K; Ma: G and I.

Differentiation
For older/more able children: Ask pairs to find speeches that are difficult to identify to test each other.
For younger/less able children: Ask the children to identify only one speech per character.

Time passes...

Objective: To investigate through reading and writing how words and phrases can signal time sequences.
What you need: Photocopiable page 18, writing materials, flipchart.

What to do
● Tell the children you are going to be looking at connectives and other words associated with time. Briefly take suggestions and list them on the flipchart. Add any common ones that may have been missed: 'first', 'then', 'after', 'meanwhile', 'from', 'where', 'at a given time' and so on.
● Discuss how there is a lot of action in *The Sheep-Pig* and that quite a bit of time passes during the story.
● Hand out photocopiable page 18. The children can work individually or in pairs. Ask them to find and underline the connectives, or words and phrases used to denote passage of time. Tell them to highlight any that occur more than once, and see if these are listed on the flipchart.
● Challenge the children to look for extracts where more than one time phrase is used: 'Half an hour later, when a beautifully clean shining Babe stood happily dripping while Hogget brushed…'
● Ask the children to substitute some of the author's words and phrases for ones of their own. Choose some children to read theirs out to the rest of the class, and discuss which are most effective and why.
● Do the children have any words to add to the list they created at the beginning of the lesson?

Differentiation
For older/more able children: Challenge the children to rewrite further sentences from the sheet, using a wide variety of time connectives. Encourage them to attempt to use a different connective or phrase each time.
For younger/less able children: Ask the children to write a list of time connectives, then use them in sentences about the characters in *The Sheep-Pig*, for example 'When Babe spoke politely, the sheep were pleased.'

Character certificates

Write certificates for Mrs Hogget, Farmer Hogget, Babe and Ma.
Think about why you are awarding the certificates, and
choose your words carefully.

This certificate is awarded to

_____

for

_____

_____

_____

_____

_____

_____

SECTION
4

"Mouthy old thing"

Mrs Hogget talks a lot! She also uses dialect and unusual expressions. Try rewriting her words in standard English. Make sure you retain the meaning.

> …got more brains than a dog he has, why 'twouldn't surprise me to hear he was rounding up them old sheep of yourn, 'twouldn't honestly, though I suppose you think I'm daft?

_____

_____

_____

> …a chap in a car seen the lorry go by in a hurry, and there's been a lot of it about, and he give the alarm, he did, kept screaming and shrieking enough to burst your eardrums, we should have lost every sheep on the place if 'tweren't for him, 'tis him we've got to thank.

_____

_____

_____

> Mouthy old thing! Some folk never know how to hold their tongues, keeping on and on about them silly gates, why don't 'e show us a picture of the spectators, might catch a glimpse of Hogget and Fly, you never knows.

_____

_____

_____

READ & RESPOND: Activities based on The Sheep-Pig

■SCHOLASTIC
www.scholastic.co.uk

SECTION
4

Who's talking?

Read the speeches. Try to work out who is saying them.
Draw lines joining the speech bubbles to the characters.

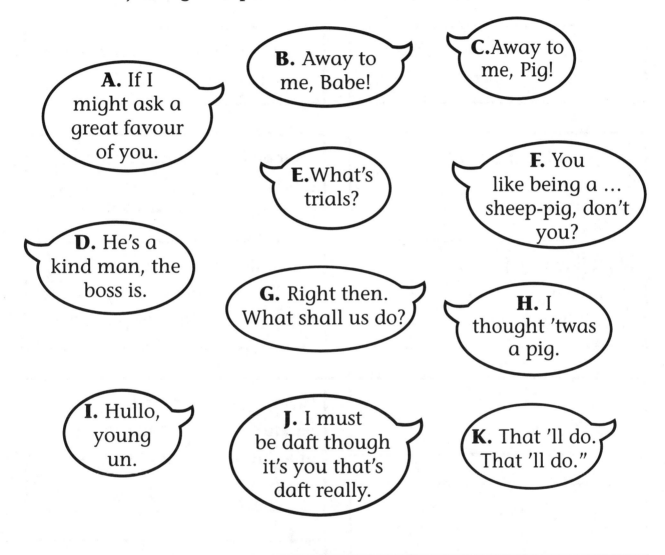

A. If I might ask a great favour of you.

B. Away to me, Babe!

C. Away to me, Pig!

E. What's trials?

F. You like being a ... sheep-pig, don't you?

D. He's a kind man, the boss is.

G. Right then. What shall us do?

H. I thought 'twas a pig.

I. Hullo, young un.

J. I must be daft though it's you that's daft really.

K. That 'll do. That 'll do."

Mrs Hogget	Babe	Fly	Farmer Hogget	Ma

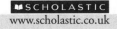

Plot, character and setting

Time passes...

Time connectives, words and phrases.
Underline the words that have an association with time.

Then, just as it seemed nothing more would happen…	When he had driven down to the village and made his delivery…
By the end of the day Babe had seen a great deal.	As soon as the Land Rover had disappeared from sight…
What happened next, later that morning in fact, was that Babe met his first sheep.	When the farmer came in for his tea, he found not only Fly but also Pig lying happily asleep…
By dark it was plain to Farmer Hogget…	Dashing across the home paddock, Babe bounded up the hill and looked about for the sheep.
As Farmer Hogget watched, a man leaned over…	
One beautiful morning, when the sky was clear and cloudless…	Half an hour later, when a beautifully clean shining Babe stood happily dripping while Hogget brushed out the tassel of his tight-curled tail…
Hogget and Babe heard the racket as they climbed the hill…	

Talk about it

How are they feeling?

> **Objective:** To discuss characters' feelings, referring to the text and making judgements.
> **What you need:** Photocopiable page 22, copies of *The Sheep-Pig*, writing materials.

What to do
● Organise the children into five groups and tell them they will be discussing Babe, Fly, Ma, Farmer Hogget and Mrs Hogget.
● First, as a class, discuss farmer Hogget's feelings. How does he feel when he first meets Babe? Do they have a bond straight away? How does he feel when he first sees Babe acting like a sheep-pig? What about when he sees him with blood on his snout? At the sheep-dog trials?
● Explain that each group member will be the expert on one of the characters. Ask the groups to decide who will be who.
● Next, ask the children to form new groups, with the other children who are experts on the same character. Hand out the photocopiable sheet to each child. Give them ten minutes to talk about the feelings of their character, making references to specific events. As they make notes on the sheet, encourage them to consider whether some of the events will affect more than one character.
● After ten minutes, tell the children to return to their 'home' group to report back.
● In a plenary session, choose a group or several individuals to report their findings. Talk about which characters change most throughout the course of the story.

> **Differentiation**
> **For older/more able children:** Ask the children to plot a graph showing how the emotions of the character change.
> **For younger/less able children:** Ask the children to draw sad, smiling or neutral faces to show how the characters feel at different points of the story.

Animals that help us

> **Objective:** To sustain conversation, explaining or giving reasons for views or choices.
> **What you need:** Copies of *The Sheep-Pig*, flipchart.

What to do
● Ask the children if their families' or friends' pets do anything out of the ordinary. Also ask the children if they have read stories of animals that have done remarkable things. Recall the extraordinary actions of Babe in *The Sheep-Pig*.
● Organise the children into groups. Ask them to talk about other tasks that dogs carry out for people, apart from herding sheep; for example, hearing dogs, and guide dogs for the blind.
● After ten minutes, ask a child from each group to report their findings to the class.
● Ask the class to suggest animals other than dogs that might be trained to help people. Record their suggestions on the flipchart. (The list could include birds, horses, elephants, donkeys and dolphins.) It is important that the children articulate why an animal is suitable for a certain task.
● Ask the children what they think is the most remarkable thing an animal does in *The Sheep-Pig*. (Babe's skills including working with the sheep and foiling the attempt to steal the sheep.)
● As a plenary, discuss as a class which is most remarkable: the tasks real animals do to help people live full lives, or the actions of the animals in the novel.

> **Differentiation**
> **For older/more able children:** Ask the children to take all the suggestions and rank them in order of importance, justifying the ranking criteria.
> **For younger/less able children:** Encourage the children to talk in pairs about the work that Babe does as a sheep-pig, explaining why he is so good at it.

Talk about it

The Sheep-Pig: the movie

Objective: To contribute to shared discussion about literature, responding to and building on the views of others.
What you need: Photocopiable page 23, copies of *The Sheep-Pig,* writing materials, flip chart.

What to do
● Tell the children that before films are made, writers have to pitch their ideas to producers.
● Ask the class to think about *The Sheep-Pig* in terms of cinema. Although it has already been made into a film, ask pairs to discuss what made it suitable for filming. Remind them that it is important that they listen, and build on each other's ideas.
● After ten minutes, hand out photocopiable page 23 to each pair to continue their discussion and make notes.

● At the end of the ten minutes ask each pair to present their 'pitch' to the rest of the class, based on their notes. Remind them to be persuasive, and round off their speech with a memorable summary or selling point. Then ask the class to vote for the best pitch.
● Establish what is dramatically interesting about *The Sheep-Pig,* and summarise the findings on the flipchart.

Differentiation
For older/more able children: The children could prepare a short radio advertisement for the film version of *The Sheep-Pig.* They will need to decide on an audience and think carefully about the persuasive language they use.
For younger/less able children: Ask the children to storyboard a short TV advertisement for *The Sheep-Pig* film, aimed at adults.

Live from the Grand Challenge Sheep Dog Trials

Objective: To present events and characters through dialogue to engage the interest of an audience.
What you need: Props such as microphones, chairs, clipboards, copies of *The Sheep-Pig,* paper, writing materials.

What to do
● Ask the children if they watch sport on the television, or listen to it on the radio. Encourage them to share their knowledge about the roles of pundit, commentator, presenter and interviewer.
● Tell the children they are going to provide a commentary for the Trials, where Babe is the final competitor.
● Invite them to take on different roles in groups of three. One will be the commentator, describing the actual events (*And now a sheep has entered the arena…*). The second will be the pundit expressing expert opinions (*Well, I don't think this is in the rules*). The third will be

the presenter in the studio, who introduces the programme and asks questions of the pundit and commentator.
● Give the groups ten minutes to prepare their programme, before presenting it to the class.
● Now ask the groups to take on new roles. One child will now be an interviewer and the other two interviewees. The interviewees could be other competitors, spectators, or even other animals taking part in the Trials. Encourage the children to use props for this part of the activity.
● Ask the groups to present their interviews to the class.

Differentiation
For older/more able children: Ask the children to work on a script for the broadcast.
For younger/less able children: Have questions prepared on clipboards. Allow longer preparation before the children present work in an assembly for the whole school.

Talk about it

"What lovely m-a-a-a-anners!"

Objective: To take different roles in groups and use language appropriate to them.
What you need: Flipchart with examples of Babe's speech and Fly's commands; paper, writing materials.

What to do

● In groups of three, give children the roles of leader, scribe and reporter. Explain that the leader will manage the activity, the scribe will write down the ideas, and the reporter will present to the rest of the class.
● Tell the children to discuss why the sheep have different attitudes to Fly (the wolf), and Babe, (the sheep-pig). After five minutes, invite the each 'reporter' to share their findings with the class.
● Next, ask the groups to suggest ways in which Fly might improve her relationship with the sheep. Allow five minutes in groups as before, then ask them to report back to the class.

● Show the examples of speech on the flipchart.
● Do the children notice what happens if the polite words are removed from Babe's speech? Ask them to discuss this in their groups.
● Next, ask them to try making the same speech more polite, and to discuss what effect this has.
● Finally, ask the children if, in the novel and in real life, they think it always pays to be polite. Is it always the way to get the best results? What do the children think is the best way for you to get them to do their work? Should they be asked or told? Hold a vote after listening to all opinions.

Differentiation
For older/more able children: The children could improvise situations in which you talk to them in a variety of different ways, and note the outcomes.
For younger/less able children: Let the children spend more time working on role plays showing the characters being polite or being rude.

In my opinion

Objective: To participate in a whole-class debate using the conventions and language of debate, including standard English.
What you need: Photocopiable page 24, writing materials.

What to do

● Remind the children of their earlier work on themes and standard English.
● Revise that the themes of a story are more than what happens and why; they are important central ideas, or wider points, about the world that the writer is making through the story. Communication is one example from *The Sheep-Pig*; what others are there? Allow two minutes' paired discussion on this before collecting ideas on the flipchart.
● Explain that you are going to hold a whole-class discussion about what the most important theme of the book is, using the conventions of a

formal debate, including standard English.
● Allow ten minutes for the pairs to make notes on the photocopiable sheet before presenting their findings to the rest of the class. They should decide which themes they think are most important, and list arguments to support this.
● Hold the debate, allowing pairs to present their arguments for the themes they think are most important, using formal language, and providing a persuasive conclusion. Allow time for questions or counter-arguments.
● When all the pairs have spoken, hold a vote to see which theme the class thinks is the most important, and discuss the result.

Differentiation
For older/more able children: Encourage the children to present their argument without the prompt sheet.
For younger/less able children: Ask the children to think of questions and counter arguments to put to the pairs presenting their arguments.

How are they feeling?

Plot how your chosen character feels at different stages in the story. Make notes on significant events that affect the character, and how he or she feels each time.

Name of character:	
Important event	**Feelings**

The Sheep-Pig: the movie

Prepare a pitch for your new film of *The Sheep-Pig*. Write notes about what is dramatic, exciting and appealing in terms of characters, action and settings.

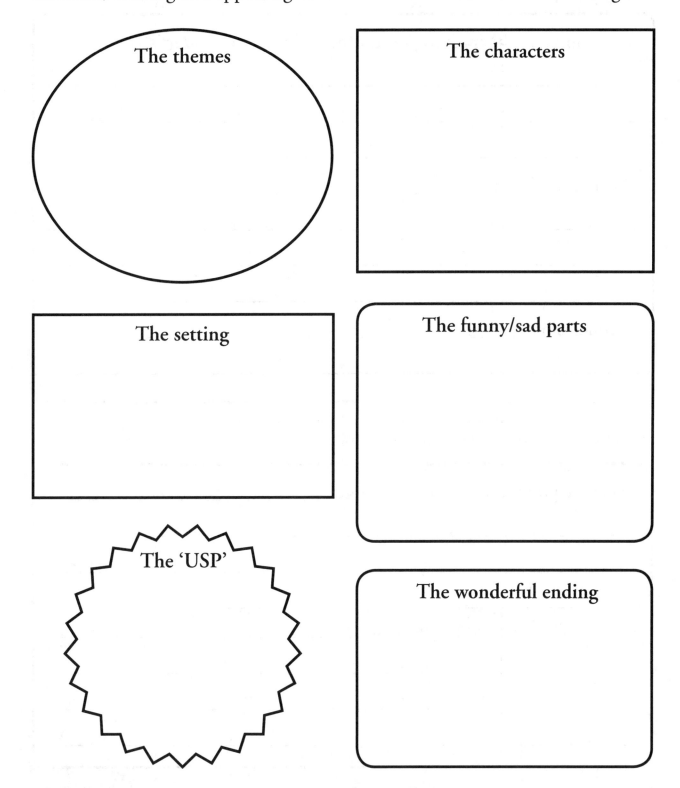

The themes

The characters

The setting

The funny/sad parts

The 'USP'

The wonderful ending

Talk about it

In my opinion

Make notes for your argument here:

In my opinion, the most important theme in *The Sheep-Pig* is _____

_____

_____

_____

I believe this because _____

_____

_____

_____

In conclusion _____

_____

Make notes on counter-arguments here:

I take the point, however I would argue _____

_____

_____

_____

I would also like to point out that _____

_____

_____

_____

Get writing

Book review

> **Objective:** To write a brief helpful review tailored for real audiences.
> **What you need:** Photocopiable page 28, copies of *The Sheep-Pig*, writing materials, flipchart.

What to do
● Explain to the class that they are going to write a review of *The Sheep-Pig* for teachers.
● Ask what information the teachers will be interested in, for example age range, subject matter and cross-curricular links, as well as the author and the length of the book. Write notes on the flipchart as the children suggest ideas.
● Next, encourage the children to think about the quality of the book. Why has the book been popular since 1983? What do they think about the book themselves? Does it have humour? Is it moving, interesting, thought-provoking?
● Hand out photocopiable page 28 to each child.

Ask the children to work in pairs for discussion, but explain that they don't need to agree about the book; they can fill in their sheets differently.
● Tell them to write their review, thinking carefully about the balance – there should be a combination of opinion and fact. Ask them to consider how much information they will give. Remind them not to give away too much of the plot, but to make sure the readers are given some enticing clues.
● Share some of the reviews and discuss them.

> **Differentiation**
> **For older/more able children:** The children should also write about why the book would be suitable for different year groups, and stick to a set word limit.
> **For younger/less able children:** Ask the children to write a bulleted list of the features of *The Sheep-Pig* under the heading 'Why you should read this book with your class'.

All about pigs

> **Objectives:** To plan, compose, edit and refine short non-chronological reports; to research and discuss topical issues, to consider social and moral dilemmas (PSHE).
> **What you need:** Flipchart, paper, writing materials.

What to do
● Tell the children they are going to write a *short* non-chronological report about pigs. Suggest they generate ideas (in their usual way – thought shower, list, mind map and so on) of relevant points from *The Sheep-Pig*, and their own knowledge about pigs.
● Work together to write a checklist of the features of reports. Mention introductions to orientate reader; use of generalisations to categorise; language to describe and differentiate; impersonal language; present tense.
● Tell the children to write in paragraphs and to bear in mind the following sections which you

could write these on the flipchart as prompts: introduction, habitat, feeding and what we get from pigs (Mrs Hogget mentions bacon, ham, pork chops, kidneys, liver, chitterlings, trotters and black pudding). They should conclude with a paragraph that discusses humans' attitudes to pigs.
● Encourage the children to be clear and concise and use an impersonal style. Start them off by suggesting that the introductory paragraph should include some basic description of pigs. Generate and display a list of topic-specific vocabulary, such as 'trotters', 'snout', 'piglets' and 'sty'.

> **Differentiation**
> **For older/more able children:** Specify an audience; perhaps a children's magazine.
> **For younger/less able children:** Write key headings about pigs, think up ideas for each and ask the children to write a sentence for each heading.

Get writing

Reporting on the Trials

> **Objective:** To write newspaper-style reports.
> **What you need:** Photocopiable page 29 for less able/younger children, copies of *The Sheep-Pig*, range of newspapers, paper, writing materials, flipchart.

What to do
● Tell the children they are going to write a newspaper report about the Sheep Dog Trials. Read Chapter 12 and ask the children to make notes of the important points.
● Next, ask them to consider what type of newspaper they will write for, and for what part – the news section or sports section. Consider what will be of interest to the reader. Ask the children to highlight their most useful notes.
● Encourage the children to think of a headline, such as 'Sheep shock' and a subheading like 'Sheep-pig steals the show at trials'. Record suggestions on the flipchart.
● Ask the children if they can remember the five Ws of journalistic writing: who, what, when, where and why. Ask the children to see how many of these they can mention in the first sentence or paragraph when they write their news story.
● Give the photocopiable sheet to those children who need the scaffold. Encourage other children to make their own mock-up of a newspaper page on which to write.
● Ask the children to write their newspaper article. Remind them that the headline and the first sentence should hook the reader. Suggest that they include quotes, perhaps from Farmer Hogget, a judge, spectators. Remind them to tie points together in a snappy conclusion.

> **Differentiation**
> **For older/more able children:** Set a tight word count. Explain that the editor will reject anything that does not fall within the limits.
> **For younger/less able children:** Ask the children to use the scaffold to plan the layout of the article.

Retelling the tale

> **Objective:** To manipulate narrative perspective by writing a story with two different narrators.
> **What you need:** Copies of *The Sheep-Pig*, flipchart.

What to do
● Ask the children who narrates *The Sheep-Pig*. (It has a neutral third-person narrator from outside the story.)
● Explain to the children that they are going to rewrite part of *The Sheep-Pig* in their own words, but with two narrators. For example, two characters could take it in turns to tell parts of the story, or one character speaks and the other makes brief asides to the reader. Write ideas on the flipchart.
● Ask the children to suggest from whose perspective *The Sheep-Pig* could be written. One option would be to alternate between a sheep-dog's and a sheep's perspective, or between Farmer Hogget and Babe.
● Whichever perspectives children choose, they should use clear, concise language that makes the story interesting for the listener. There should be an obvious distinction between the two 'voices'.
● Let the pairs choose scenes for retelling themselves, and give them some discussion time before they begin writing.
● Share the new versions in large groups or as a whole class.

> **For older/more able children:** Ask the children to include a minor character, such as one of the sheep.
> **For younger/less able children:** Suggest that the children stick to the main characters. Help them to maintain the chosen point of view.

Get writing

At home with the Hoggets

> **Objective:** To write character portraits and present them in a variety of ways.
> **What you need:** Celebrity lifestyle magazines, paper, writing materials, flipchart.

What to do
- Talk about and show some of the magazines, reading brief excerpts.
- Tell the children that, after Babe's success at the Trials, Farmer and Mrs Hogget have become famous and now many people want to interview them, including a celebrity lifestyle magazine.
- Discuss key features of the Hoggets' lifestyle as indicated in the novel, for example, details of their house, personalities and appearance, and record these on the flipchart. (Farmer Hogget driving his Land Rover, Mrs Hogget making cakes, jams, pickles and preserves for the Home Produce stall, and so on.)

- Model some example sentences, demonstrating the chatty tone the article should achieve, for example, 'No one was more surprised than Mrs Hogget when she watched her husband and his pig win the Trials.'
- Ask the children to browse the book to make notes before they write the article. The finished piece should be an interview with an introductory paragraph, and a conclusion about the Hoggets' future. Encourage the children to use the book, but also to have fun imagining answers to interview questions. Mrs Hogget's replies will be very long, Farmer Hogget's probably one word.

> **Differentiation**
> **For older/more able children:** Set a tight word limit.
> **For younger/less able children:** Ask the children to draw pictures of the Hoggets on the farm and add magazine-type captions.

Story to script

> **Objective:** To write a playscript, using a known story as the basis; to take part in drama.
> **What you need:** Photocopiable page 30, writing materials, flipchart.

What to do
- Ask the children what they can remember about the features of a playscript, such as: characters' names appear at the left followed by colon; stage directions should be included; setting details given at beginning of scene and elsewhere as appropriate. Record these points on the flipchart.
- Hand out photocopiable page 30 and explain to the class that they will be adapting the extract as part of a playscript.
- Read through the extract together, noting where the scene takes place, then establish which characters are involved.

- Now ask the children to underline the dialogue in the extract. (You may need to remind them to look for speech marks or signifiers such as 'said'.) Encourage them to annotate the text for events that could be developed dramatically and to cross through details that can be omitted from a staged production.
- Ask the children to write their scenes, using script conventions. Encourage early finishers to try out each other's scripts in groups of three (there are four characters but Fly has no lines).
- As a plenary, discuss what is dramatic about this extract and about *The Sheep-Pig* in general.

> **Differentiation**
> **For older/more able children:** Encourage the children to write director's notes in the margins about how to stage the scene.
> **For younger/less able children:** Ask the children to write dialogue, without adding stage directions.

Get writing

Book Review

Use these different sections to plan your review of *The Sheep-Pig*.

Why do you like *The Sheep-Pig*?

_____
_____
_____
_____
_____
_____
_____
_____
_____
_____
_____
_____

What is your favourite part?

_____
_____
_____
_____
_____
_____
_____
_____
_____
_____
_____
_____
_____
_____
_____
_____
_____

Why would teachers find *The Sheep-Pig* useful?

_____
_____
_____
_____
_____
_____
_____
_____

Length of book:

_____
_____

Age range:

_____
_____
_____

Reporting on the Trials

headline

subheading

article here

photograph
here

caption here

byline (name of reporter)

who, what, where, when, why, summary

Get writing

Story to script

Mrs Hogget even took to calling Babe to the back door, to feed him some titbit or other that she thought he might particularly fancy; and from here it was but a short step to inviting him into the house, which one day she did.

When the farmer came in for his tea, he found not only Fly but also Pig lying happily asleep beside the Aga cooker. And afterwards, when he sat down in his armchair in the sitting-room and switched on the television, Babe came to sit beside him, and they watched the six o'clock news together.

"He likes it," said Hogget to his wife when she came into the room. Mrs Hogget nodded her head a great many times, and as usual had a few words to say on the subject.

"Dear little chap, though you can't call him little no longer, he've growed so much, why, he's big enough to you-know-what, not that we ever shall now, over my dead body though I hopes it ain't if you see what I do mean, just look at him, we should have brought him in the house long ago, no reason why not, is there now?"

"He might mess the carpet," said Farmer Hogget.

"Never!" cried Mrs Hogget, shaking her head the entire time she was speaking. "He's no more likely to mess than he is to fly, he'll ask to go out when he wants to do his do's, just like a good clean dog would, got more brains than a dog he has, why 'twouldn't surprise me to hear he was rounding up them old sheep of yourn, 'twouldn't honestly, though I suppose you think I'm daft?"

Farmer Hogget grinned to himself.

Assessment

Assessment advice

You will have been assessing and monitoring pupil progress throughout the study of *The Sheep-Pig*, in both formal and informal ways.

The assessment activity below is suitable for children across Key Stage 2, and should be seen as another part of the study of the novel, and not the overall aim. Formative assessment should have been taking place throughout the study of the book.

This assessment should be seen as part of a cycle, and whatever conclusions you reach when marking will hopefully be carried forward into helping the children enjoy and learn from the next book they study. Similarly, your existing knowledge of the children should inform how you approach the delivery and marking of this task.

For most teachers and children, then, the assessment will be *for* learning – to set targets, monitor progress and so on. For some children (especially in Year 6) it may also be assessment *of* learning, where it will be useful for you to know at what level the children are working. The aim in both cases should be to encourage and nurture effective, independent learners.

My life on the farm

What you need: Photocopiable page 32, writing materials.

What to do
● Tell the children they are going to write a monologue given by Babe to a pig that he has just met, describing his life on the farm as a sheep-pig. It is the eve of the Grand Challenge Sheep Dog Trials.
● Explain that Babe's speech should focus mainly on his feelings about the tournament tomorrow. Is he nervous? Excited? How has his practice been going? Encourage the children to include a brief description of the farm, along with details about the people and animals he has met. Although Babe does most of the talking, the children should also make notes of the kind of questions the other pig might want to ask him, for instance: How did he become a sheep-pig? Is he happy on the farm? What are his hopes for the future?
● Tell the children you will be looking for quality of descriptive writing, including the appropriate use of adjectives, powerful verbs, adverbs and figurative language; and features of informal speech, such as chatty language and a conversational tone.
● Hand out the photocopiable sheet (making copies beforehand, without the prompts, for more able children) and ask the children to work individually to write Babe's speech.

Differentiation
For older/more able children: The children could incorporate Babe's speech into a piece of dialogue, incorporating the other pig's questions and Babe's responses.
For younger/less able children: The template provides a reassuring scaffold, and can be enlarged for those with larger handwriting.

My life on the farm

It is the night before the Grand Challenge Sheep Dog Trials. Imagine you are Babe. Write down what you would say to a pig you have just met about your life on the farm and the Sheep Dog Trials tomorrow.

When I arrived on the farm

> Remember to describe the animals and people.

I became interested in being a Sheep-Pig when

> Don't forget to say what you have been doing and what you hope to do in the future.

> Have you written about the farm?

I feel

> Are you happy?

about the Sheep Dog Trials tomorrow.

SCHOLASTIC
www.scholastic.co.uk